Nina's Shells

Written by Carolyn Lee
Illustrated by Lloyd Foye

Nina likes to find shells
at the beach.

2

3

She has white shells
and brown shells.

5

She has smooth shells
and bumpy shells.

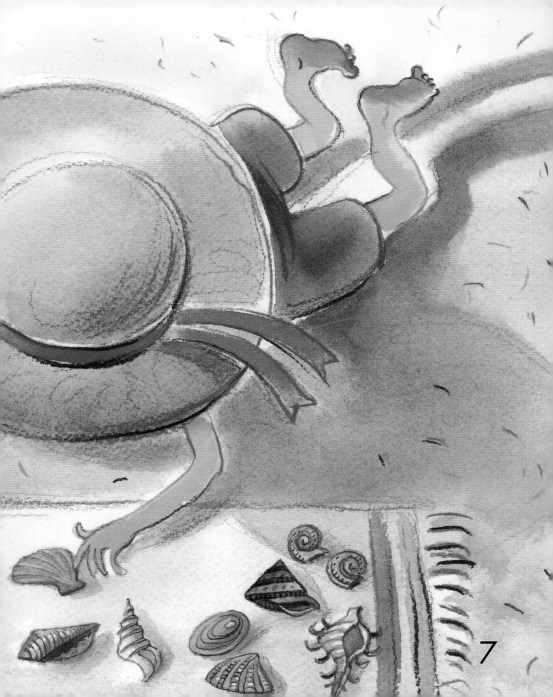

She has shells of many shapes and sizes.

But she needs one more special shell.

She finds a smooth, white rock.
She wants to keep it.
But it is not a shell.

She finds some wet seaweed.
She throws it into the water.
It is not a shell.

She finds a green shovel.
She likes it.
But it is not a shell.

She sees something
white and round.
It has a star on it.
Is it a shell?

15

Yes!
It is a special shell.
Now Nina has a whole
collection.